This book belongs to:
_____

30 Day SPIRITUAL WARFARE Prayer Journal

Dr. Priscilla Akins

30 Day Spiritual Warfare Prayer Journal

Copyright © 2021 Priscilla Akins
All Rights Reserved.

ISBN 978-1-7353091-5-6

In accordance, with the U.S. Copyright Act of 1976, scanning, uploading, reproducing, storing in an electronic system, or transmitted in any form or by any means, electronic, mechanical, photocopy, recording, or otherwise without prior written permission from the author constitutes unlawful piracy and theft of the author's intellectual property. Brief quotations may be used in a literary review. Short quotations or occasional page copying for personal or group study is permitted and encouraged; permission will be granted upon request.

Although every precaution has been taken to verify the accuracy of the information contain herein, the author and publisher assumes no responsibility for any errors or omissions. No liability is assumed for any liability, loss, risk, personal or otherwise, which is incurred as a consequence, directly or indirectly, of the use and application of any of the contents of this book.

Unless otherwise noted, Scripture notations are taken from the
King James Version of the Bible.

Edited:
Glenda Wright

Proofread:
Ruby Porter

Cover and Interior Layout & Design:
Tarsha L. Campbell

Published by:
DOMINIONHOUSE
Publishing & Design, LLC
P.O. Box 681938 | Orlando, Florida 32868
407.703.4800 phone
www.mydominionhouse.com

The Lord gave the Word: great was the company
of those who published it. (Psalms 68:11)

Dedication

This book is dedicated in memory of my beloved mother, Missionary Lonnie Bell Daniels, whose love, guidance, and prayer life greatly influenced me. Thank you, Mother, for all that you imparted in my life. Love you forever.

"If you long to be a mighty warrior, to do great things for the Lord, and to win the world for him, then remember that your power is in your prayer life."

-Sunday Adelaja

Acknowledgements

"Giving thanks, praise and all glory to GOD. Grace be unto you and peace from GOD our Father, and from the Lord Jesus Christ. I thank my GOD upon remembrance of you. Always in every prayer of mine for you all making requests with joy for your fellowship in the gospel from the first day until now." Philippians 1:1-5.

I want to acknowledge my leaders, Bishop Alva D. Harris and Pastor Ida Harris, Deliverance Temple Global Ministries for their prayers and support.

I acknowledge New Hope Outreach Deliverance Ministries. Thank you for your prayers and support. To all of my family and loved ones that prayed for me and supported me, thank you.

I acknowledge all of my friends, far and near, who prayed for me faithfully and encouraged me. Thank you.

To Prophetess Tarsha Campbell, author, publisher, and certified coach, who advised me until the end, I appreciate you and the faithful dedication to the call of GOD upon your life. Thank you.

"The true prayer, spends more time with the commander and less time in the battle."

-Don Miller

Table of Contents

Introduction 13

A Prayer Warrior's Prayer 15

Day 1
I Bow Before You, Father 17

Day 2
Praying in the Authority of Jesus' Name. 23

Day 3
Appreciating and Recognizing the Father's Love . . . 29

Day 4
Knowing and Declaring the Will of God for Your Life
. . . . 35

Day 5
Walking in the Victory of the Lord Jesus Christ . . . 41

Day 6
Total Surrender, I Surrender All 47

Day 7
Praying for Spiritual Alertness and Spiritual Insight . 53

Day 8
Standing on the Truth of God's Word 59

Day 9
Thanking God for His Divine Protection 65

Day 10
Walking in the Fullness of God's Will Today 71

Day 11
Declaring and Decreeing God's Word Over My Life . 77

Table of Contents

Day 12
Living in the Power of Jesus Christ's Resurrection . . 83

Day 13
Walking in Your Spirit, Yielding to Your Love 89

Day 14
Being Empowered by the Holy Spirit 95

Day 15
Taking a Stand 101

Day 16
Just Speak to It 107

Day 17
Because You Are My Shepherd 113

Day 18
The Importance of True Fellowship 119

Day 19
Walking in the Blessings and Living in the Blessings 125

Day 20
Being Made Whole in His Presence 131

Day 21
Prayer of Release 137

Day 22
Staying Focused 143

Day 23
Being and Staying Militant: Ready for Battle 149

Table of Contents

Day 24
Walking in Pureness of Heart by the Power of the
Holy Spirit 155

Day 25
Taking a Stand in the Midst of Adversity 161

Day 26
Taking Courage. 167

Day 27
Staying Calm 173

Day 28
Receiving a Fresh Outpouring of Your Spirit 179

Day 29
Knowing God in the Power of His Might 185

Day 30
Being Persistent in Spiritual Warfare
During Trials 191

About the Author. 196

Our Prayer Ministry 198

Contact the Author. 199

"Worship is how we express our love, adoration and wonder at God's presence. The Christian breathes in God's goodness and exhale in worship."

-A. W. Tozier

Introduction

The Essentials of the Prayer Warrior

Warfare is powerful. A prayer warrior must read the Word of God and pray for all men everywhere.

(1 Timothy 2:1-3)

....

We must maintain balance as a prayer warrior. We must love from a pure heart and a clean conscience, have sincere faith, and expect God to move.

Be filled with the Holy Ghost.

Keep safe that which has been entrusted to you, as we receive this call to prayer.

Read 1 Timothy 6:20 from the King James Version below.

"O Timothy, keep that which is committed to thy trust, avoiding profane and vain babbling, and oppositions of science falsely so called:"

We have our battles daily. These prayers are taken from scripture and written through the power of the Holy Spirit, the ultimate intercessor, as we declare and decree God's spoken Word daily over our lives, our families, jobs, bodies, and finances. We experience this peace of God in every situation, no matter what it involves, just knowing that God has given us power and authority through His Word to dismantle the plans of the enemy. Before our day begins, Psalms 63:1 reads, "O God, thou art my God; early will I seek thee: my soul thirsteth for thee, my flesh longeth for thee in a dry and thirsty land, where no water is;"

I pray that these prayers strengthen, encourage, and give you faith, knowing that you have the victory in the name of Jesus.

***

Introduction

A Prayer Warrior's Prayer

***

A warrior of prayer is called to be dressed and armed for the enemy.

Today, I am dressed and claim victory by putting on the armor God has designed for me.

I put on the girdle of truth, for it's on His Word that I must stand. All other ground is sinking sand.

I put on the breastplate of righteousness, through Jesus Christ that can only be,

I am in Him, and He's in me.

My feet are shod with the preparation of the gospel of peace, that I may carry His Word far and near for the men, women, boys, and girls to hear.

I take the shield of faith, and I hold it up against every fiery dart of the enemy that will come against me today.

I cannot do this on my own. With faith in God I'm never alone.

I put on the helmet of salvation. My identity in Christ is secure.

Keep my mind focused today on Your Word; and my foundation is sure.

I take the sword of the spirit, Your Word; in my hands to cut the enemy's head–cut him long and continuously. This, I will do to destroy the enemy's plan.

A warrior, that's me, dressed, armed, and ready for the enemy.

"O' Come let us worship

and bow down

let us kneel before

the Lord our maker."

-Psalms 95:6

Day 1

I Bow Before You, Father

"God is a Spirit: and they that worship him must worship him in spirit and in truth."

(John 4:24, King James Version)

- -

To bow is to worship. The Hebrew word for bow means to worship.

"God is a Spirit: and they that worship him must worship him in spirit and in truth." Your heart must be sincere.

Prayer:

Heavenly Father,

I thank You for the opportunity You have given me to bow before You. I welcome Your presence, and I come in humility, asking You to cleanse and purify me. I realize I must come with a pure heart and clean hands. Intensify the desire within me to want more of You. Crucify my flesh for they that worship You must worship You in spirit and in truth.

I totally surrender myself to You. Take control of my thoughts. I refuse to allow the enemy to cloud my mind today with negative thoughts. I cast down every vain imagination in Jesus' name. As I enter, into Your presence, I open my heart to receive Your peace, love, and joy. Fill me with all the fullness of You, endowing me with Your power as I worship You. Empower me to say what heaven is saying, being in tune with the angels. You are Alpha and Omega, the beginning and the end. To Him be all glory, dominion, and power, both now and forevermore. I worship and adore You as I bow before You.

In Jesus' name,

Amen

Questions

_____
_____
_____
_____
_____
_____
_____

What God Revealed to Me

_____
_____
_____
_____
_____
_____
_____

30 Day Spiritual Warfare Prayer Journal

Scriptures

_____

_____

_____

_____

_____

_____

What God Revealed to Me

_____

_____

_____

_____

_____

_____

_____

_____

I Bow Before You, Father

Concerns I Have to Pray About

"If thou art bound by sickness, If sorrows weary thee, If thou art trembling with fear invoke the name of Jesus."

-St. Lawrence Justinian, 1381-1456

Day 2

Praying in the Authority of Jesus' Name

"Behold, I give unto you power to tread on serpents and scorpions, and over all the power of the enemy: and nothing shall by any means hurt you."

(Luke 10:19, King James Version)

There is power in the authority of Jesus' name. He has given us His name to use against every satanic attack that comes against us.

Prayer:

Heavenly Father,

I thank You for Your Son, Jesus, and the power of the cross. Thank You for the power of His name. For it is strength and power, my refuge. I can run into it, and I am safe. In the name of Jesus and by the power of His blood, Satan, I bind you. I dismantle every plan and effort of attack against my family, my body, my mind, and emotions in any way. You are a defeated foe; you were defeated at the cross, and you are defeated in my life. In the authority of Jesus' name, I command every spirit that you have assigned to me to bring fear and discouragement of any kind to go now! In Jesus' name go where Jesus ordered you to go in the dry places and never return.

Amen

Praying in the Authority of Jesus' Name

Questions

_____
_____
_____
_____
_____
_____
_____

What God Revealed to Me

_____
_____
_____
_____
_____
_____
_____
_____

30 Day Spiritual Warfare Prayer Journal

Scriptures

_____

_____

_____

_____

_____

_____

What God Revealed to Me

_____

_____

_____

_____

_____

_____

_____

_____

PRAYING IN THE AUTHORITY OF JESUS' NAME

Concerns I Have to Pray About

"Understand that GOD is always faithful in his love for you."

-Karen Middleton

Day 3

Appreciating, Recognizing, and Accepting the Father's Love

*"The Lord hath appeared of old unto me, saying,
Yea, I have loved thee with an everlasting love:
therefore with lovingkindness have I drawn thee."*

(Jeremiah 31:3, King James Version)

To know the love of God toward us is amazing. Even when we were yet sinners, He proved His love for us (Romans 5:8).

Prayer:

Heavenly Father,

I thank You for the love that You have shown to me, giving Your only begotten Son that I would have a right to eternal life. You have loved me with an everlasting love. Even when I was in my sins, You loved me. I am thankful for all of Your promises. Thank You for Your mercy, grace, faithfulness, and the assurance I'm never alone. You are always with me, even to the end of the world. Today, help me to recognize

Your love for me in every way. I thank You, Father, that all I need is in You. Thank You for being my shelter, my refuge, and the horn of my salvation. Help me to appreciate Your love daily in every area of my life.

In Jesus' name,

Amen

✳✳✳

When I'm feeling unloved and alone:

1. Read **Jeremiah 31:3-4, Romans 5:8, 1 John 4:7-8.** Study and meditate on these scriptures.

2. Discover God's love for you, read **1 John 4:7-20.**

3. Grow closer to God by knowing His love and kindness toward you by studying **Jeremiah 31:3.**

4. God's love and kindness is better that life itself. Meditate on **Psalms 63:3.**

God's love for you is better than life itself. Begin to pray the love scriptures, and you will begin to see and feel the love of God in your life, which will empower your walk with Christ.

**APPRECIATING, RECOGNIZING,
AND ACCEPTING THE FATHER'S LOVE**

Questions

_____
_____
_____
_____
_____
_____
_____

What God Revealed to Me

_____
_____
_____
_____
_____
_____
_____
_____

30 Day Spiritual Warfare Prayer Journal

Scriptures

What God Revealed to Me

APPRECIATING, RECOGNIZING,
AND ACCEPTING THE FATHER'S LOVE

Concerns I Have to Pray About

_____

_____

_____

_____

_____

_____

_____

_____

_____

_____

_____

_____

_____

_____

_____

_____

_____

"There is no if's in GOD's world, and no places that are safer than other places. The center of His will is our only safety. Let us pray that we may know it."

-Corrie Ten Boom

Day 4

Knowing and Declaring the Will of God For Your Life

"And be not conformed to this world: but be ye transformed by the renewing of your mind that ye may prove what is that good, and perfect, will of God."

(Romans 12:2, King James Version)

We know the will of God through reading His Word, meditating on His Word, praying, decreeing, and declaring His Word over our lives, our families, our finances, and our ministries.

Prayer:

Heavenly Father,

I give You praise today that I can know Your perfect will for my life through the promises of Your word. I know that Your thoughts toward me are good and not evil. I decree and declare that I will experience and know Your peace in every area of my life. I decree and declare that according to Your promises I will prosper and be in good health even as my soul prospers. I bind you, Satan, in the name of Jesus, and every attack that you bring against the perfect will of God in my life. My life is hidden in Christ Jesus through God. You will not hinder the plan and purpose of God in my life. I command every spirit that you have assigned to interrupt the will of God in my life to leave. Go to the dry places where Jesus ordered you to go and never return. I thank You, Father, as I walk in obedience to Your word that everything You have planned for my life will be manifested.

In the name of Jesus,
Amen

**KNOWING AND DECLARING
THE WILL OF GOD FOR YOUR LIFE**

Questions

_____
_____
_____
_____
_____
_____
_____

What God Revealed to Me

_____
_____
_____
_____
_____
_____
_____

Scriptures

What God Revealed to Me

**KNOWING AND DECLARING
THE WILL OF GOD FOR YOUR LIFE**

Concerns I Have to Pray About

"Jesus gave you authority, but it is up to you to walk in it. (Paul Balius) Jesus said, Behold, I give you authority to trample on serpents and scorpions and over all the power of the enemy."

-Luke 10:19

Day 5

Walking in the Victory of the Lord Jesus Christ

"But thanks be to God, which giveth us the victory through our Lord Jesus Christ."

(1 Corinthians 15:57, Kings James Version)

....

We must walk in the victory of Jesus Christ, proclaiming His Word in every situation we encounter.

"Yet in all these things we are more than conquerors through him who loved us" (Romans 8:37).

Prayer:

Heavenly Father,

I thank You for the victory that You won for me at Calvary's cross. Today, I walk in that victory, knowing that no weapon formed against me shall prosper. Through that victory, my family is saved, set free, and delivered in Jesus' name. I have the mind of Christ; I pull down every vain imagination and bring every thought into captivity that's not of God. The battle has already been won. The weapons of my warfare are not carnal but mighty through God. In the name of Jesus, I pull down every stronghold of Satan. I command you to loose your hold. I am victorious in every area of my life today,

In Jesus' name,

Amen

WALKING IN THE VICTORY OF THE LORD JESUS CHRIST

Questions

_____
_____
_____
_____
_____
_____
_____

What God Revealed to Me

_____
_____
_____
_____
_____
_____
_____
_____

Scriptures

_____
_____
_____
_____
_____
_____

What God Revealed to Me

_____
_____
_____
_____
_____
_____
_____
_____

**WALKING IN THE VICTORY OF THE
LORD JESUS CHRIST**

Concerns I Have to Pray About

"What we really need is only a heart of surrender and always trust what GOD has planned for our life. So we do our best, GOD shall take care of the rest. That's what I call faith."

-Olivia Singa

Day 6

Total Surrender, I Surrender All

"I beseech you therefore, brethren, by the mercies of God, that ye present your bodies a living sacrifice, holy, acceptable unto God, which is your reasonable service."

(Romans 12:1, King James Version)

Surrender your whole heart, body, and soul to God. God wants all of you.

Prayer:

I thank You, Heavenly Father, for Your tender mercy. Unto thee O Lord, do I lift up my soul (Psalms 25:1, KJV). Examine me O Lord, search me, and know my heart. I surrender all to You. I come before You casting all of my burdens, for I know You care for me. Take away all of my pain, sorrow, and grief. Cleanse my heart and have mercy upon me O God, according to thy love and kindness. Fill me up God with more of You and less of me. All of You and none of me. Satan, I bind you in the name of Jesus. I am the temple of God, and I command you in the power of Jesus name to loose your hold on me. I have the mind of Christ. Go! In Jesus' name go where Jesus ordered you to go to, to the dry places and never return. Father, I thank You for Your faithfulness. My soul waiteth upon You. My expectation is of You. Thank You, Father, for making me over again and removing everything out of my life that's not pleasing to You.

In Jesus' name,

Amen

Questions

_____
_____
_____
_____
_____
_____
_____

What God Revealed to Me

_____
_____
_____
_____
_____
_____
_____
_____

Scriptures

_____

_____

_____

_____

_____

_____

What God Revealed to Me

_____

_____

_____

_____

_____

_____

_____

_____

Concerns I Have to Pray About

"Be sober, be vigilant; because your adversary the devil, as a roaring lion, walketh about seeking whom he may devour."

-1 Peter 5:8

Day 7

Praying for Spiritual Alertness and Spiritual Insight

"Lest Satan should get an advantage of us: for we are not ignorant of his devices."

(2 Corinthians 2:11, King James Version)

We must stay spiritually awake and alert in order to discern the tactics of the enemy.

Prayer:

Heavenly Father,

I thank You for this day as I enter into this prayer. I pray that the God of our Lord, Jesus Christ, the Father of glory may give unto me the spirit of wisdom and revelation in the knowledge of Him that my spiritual eyes of understanding will be enlightened. I pray that I will able to discern every tactic and device of the enemy.

Holy Spirit, open my ears that I will hear Your voice and follow You as You lead me in the way to go. Therefore, on this day, I cancel every plan of the enemy that's been formed against me. In Jesus' name, I will be alert through the power of the Holy Spirit.

Amen

PRAYING FOR SPIRITUAL ALERTNESS AND SPIRITUAL INSIGHT

Questions

What God Revealed to Me

30 Day Spiritual Warfare Prayer Journal

Scriptures

_____
_____
_____
_____
_____
_____

What God Revealed to Me

_____
_____
_____
_____
_____
_____
_____
_____

Praying for Spiritual Alertness and Spiritual Insight

Concerns I Have to Pray About

"Heaven and earth will pass away,

but my word will not pass away."

-Matthew 24:35

Day 8

Standing on the Truth of God's Word

"Heaven and the earth shall pass away, but my words shall not pass away."

(Matthew 24:35, King James Version).

....

God's Word is true. We can stand on the promises of God regardless of the circumstances we face daily. When God could not swear by anyone else, He swore by Himself. His Word is settled in heaven.

Prayer:

Heavenly Father,

I thank You for Your word because all of Your promises are yea and amen (2 Corinthians 1:20, KJV). I stand on Your word today, thanking and praising You for loving me. I give thanks that You are my strength, for in Your strength I find joy and experience the peace promised in Your word. I will walk in divine health (3 John 2, KJV). I thank You, Father, that Your word is settled in heaven. I thank You that You already have a plan for me, and I stand on Your word.

I thank You for Your faithfulness to me, supplying my every need according to Your riches in glory. All of my needs are met today because You are my shepherd, and I shall not want.

In Jesus' name,

Amen

Questions

What God Revealed to Me

Scriptures

What God Revealed to Me

Concerns I Have to Pray About

"The Lord will keep you from all harm. He will watch over your life. The Lord will watch over you coming and going both now and forever more."

-Psalm 127:7-8

Day 9

Thanking God for His Divine Protection

"The God of my rock: in him will I trust; he is my shield, and the horn of my salvation, my high tower, and my refuge, my saviour; thou savest me from violence."

(2 Samuel 22:3, King James Version)

God is our protection from things seen and unseen. He watches over us for He cares for us.

Prayer:

Dear Heavenly Father,

I thank You that You are my rock, and in You I trust. Thank You for being my shield and buckler, the Lord of my salvation, my high tower and my refuge.

Thank You for Your name. I can run into it, and I know that I'm safe. I thank You for Your angels that encamp around those who fear You. I will say that You are my refuge and my fortress.

You are my God; a thousand shall fall at my side and ten thousand at my right hand. But it shall not come nigh unto me. No weapon formed against me shall prosper because I am Your servant.

I thank You, Father, for Your divine protection today.

In Jesus' name,

Amen

**THANKING GOD FOR HIS
DIVINE PROTECTION**

Questions

_____
_____
_____
_____
_____
_____
_____

What God Revealed to Me

_____
_____
_____
_____
_____
_____
_____
_____

Scriptures

_____
_____
_____
_____
_____
_____

What God Revealed to Me

_____
_____
_____
_____
_____
_____
_____
_____

**THANKING GOD FOR HIS
DIVINE PROTECTION**

Concerns I Have to Pray About

"Those who walk with GOD always reach their destination."

-Henry Ford

Day 10

Walking in the Fullness of God's Will Today

"And hath put all things under his feet, and gave him to be the head over all things to the church, which is his body, the fullness of him that filleth all in all."

(Ephesians 1:22-23, King James Version)

Walking in the fullness of God's will is my desire. I claim the fullness of the will of God for my life today.

Prayer:

Heavenly Father,

I thank You for power. I ask You to fill me with all the fullness of You today. As I walk in the fullness of You, I yield to You in every area of my life. I thank You this day for transforming me into Your likeness, changing my character, leading, guiding, and instructing me in the way. You would have me to go. Teach me Lord, the way of Your statues that I may follow to the end. Give me understanding, that I may keep

Your laws. Direct me in the path of Your commands, for there I find delight (Psalms 119: 22-35, KJV).

In Jesus' name,

Amen

***Walking in the Fullness of
God's Will Today***

Questions

_____
_____
_____
_____
_____
_____
_____

What God Revealed to Me

_____
_____
_____
_____
_____
_____
_____
_____

Scriptures

_____

_____

_____

_____

_____

What God Revealed to Me

_____

_____

_____

_____

_____

_____

_____

_____

**WALKING IN THE FULLNESS OF
GOD'S WILL TODAY**

Concerns I Have to Pray About

"You will also decree a thing, and it will be established for you; so light will shine upon your ways."

Job 22:28 (NKJV)

Day 11

Declaring and Decreeing God's Word Over My Life

"Thou shalt also decree a thing, and it shall be established unto thee: and the light shall shine upon thy ways."

(Job 22:28, King James Version)

Whatever I decree in Jesus' name shall come to pass.

Prayer:

Heavenly Father,

You are my refuge and my rock. You are in control of everything that happens in my life. Satan, by the authority of Jesus' name, I decree your works in my life are destroyed. I decree God's Word over my life.

I shall walk in divine healing, according to His Word that declares "I am the Lord that heals" (Exodus 15:26). I decree that I will be the head and not the tail (Deuteronomy 28:13).

I decree salvation for my family, children, and love ones (Acts 16:31). I decree the peace of God, and I decree the strength of God for today. I decree the joy of the Lord.

I shall walk in prosperity according to your Word (3 John 3:1-2). I decree that I am blessed going out and blessed coming in; my blessings shall run me down and overtake me (Deuteronomy 28:2).

I decree that everything I put my hands to and do in Your name shall prosper and be blessed.

I decree that God will be with me in everything I do according to His will for my life to prosper me. His thoughts toward me are good, and I am precious in His sight. He is able to complete and finish the work He has begun in me. I thank You, Lord.

In Jesus' name,

Amen

**DECLARING AND DECREEING
GOD'S WORD OVER MY LIFE**

Questions

_____
_____
_____
_____
_____
_____
_____

What God Revealed to Me

_____
_____
_____
_____
_____
_____
_____
_____

Scriptures

What God Revealed to Me

***Declaring and Decreeing
God's Word Over My Life***

Concerns I Have to Pray About

"The resurrection gives my life meaning and direction and the opportunity to start over no matter what my 'circumstances.'"

-Henry Knox Sherril

Day 12

Living in the Power of Jesus Christ's Resurrection

"For if we have been planted together in the likeness of his death, we shall be also in the likeness of his resurrection."

(Romans 6:5, King James Version)

There is power in the resurrection of Jesus Christ, and His desire is for us to know that we can live in that power.

Prayer:

Heavenly Father,

I thank You for the work of the cross and the power of the blood of Jesus. I thank You for it was at Calvary's cross that the victory was won. Because of the work at Calvary's cross, I can cast all of my burdens, sorrows, and pain upon You. I will no longer walk in sin and shame, for I am a new creature in Christ, and old things are passed away. I no longer live, but Christ lives through me, so I mortify the deeds of the flesh through the power of the resurrection of the cross. Through the power of the Holy Spirit, I put off the works of the flesh: adultery, fornication, uncleanness, lasciviousness, idolatry, witchcraft, hatred, variance, emulation, wrath, strife, sedition, heresies, envying, murders, drunkenness, and reveling. The fruit of the spirit will be manifested through me: meekness, temperance, love, joy, peace, longsuffering, gentleness, goodness, against such there is no law, and they that are Christ's have crucified the flesh with affection and lust (Galatians 5:20-21, KJV). I will live in the power of Jesus Christ and His resurrection.

In Jesus' name,

Amen

Questions

What God Revealed to Me

Scriptures

What God Revealed to Me

Concerns I Have to Pray About

"If we live by the spirit, let us also walk by the spirit."

-Galatians 5:25

***

"It is the spirit that gives life: The flesh profits nothing."

-John 6:63

Day 13

Walking in Your Spirit, Yielding to Your Love

This I say then, Walk in the Spirit, and ye shall not fulfill the lust of the flesh.

(Galatians 5:16, King James Version)

When we walk in the Spirit, we will have a fruitful life in our walk with the Lord as well as a committed relationship.

Prayer:

Heavenly Father,

I thank You for Your Holy Spirit that abides within me as my day begins. I yield to Your Spirit, and as He enables me to walk according to Your word, Your love is manifested. This lets me know that no matter what comes my way the love of God through the power of His Spirit will keep me and cause me not to yield to the lusts of the flesh. Satan, I bind you in the name of Jesus. You will not cause me to doubt God's love for me in any way today. His love is unconditional and everlasting. I yield to God's love that surrounds me in every aspect of my life. There is no love like the Father's love. I thank You, Father, for Your Spirit, as I yield to Your love.

In Jesus' name,

Amen

Questions

What God Revealed to Me

Scriptures

What God Revealed to Me

Concerns I Have to Pray About

"I pray that out of his glorious riches he may strengthen you with power through his spirit in your inner being."

-Ephesians 3:16

Day 14

Being Empowered by the Holy Spirit

"But ye shall receive power, after that the Holy Ghost is come upon you: and ye shall be witnesses unto me both in Jerusalem, and in all Judea, and in Samaria, and unto the uttermost part of the earth."

(Acts 1:8, King James Version)

We must desire to be filled with all the fullness of the Spirit and proven to the will of the Father.

Prayer:

Heavenly Father,

I am grateful for the power of Your Holy Spirit. Endow me with power, so that I will be able to stand against the wiles of the enemy. I thank You for Your power, for it's by Your power that change comes into my life. Continuously, take over my mind and help me to think on whatsoever things are true, whatsoever things are pure, whatsoever things are lovely, and whatsoever things are of good report. If there be any virtue, if there be any praise through the power of Your Spirit. I will think on these things (Philippians 4:8, KJV). Satan, I bind you jn the name of Jesus. You will not fill my mind with negative thoughts concerning anything that I may encounter. I plead the blood of Jesus over my mind, my emotions, and my body. I command you to leave and go to the dry places where Jesus ordered you to go, in Jesus' name. I will operate in the power of the Holy Spirit.

Amen

Questions

What God Revealed to Me

30 Day Spiritual Warfare Prayer Journal

Scriptures

_____
_____
_____
_____
_____
_____

What God Revealed to Me

_____
_____
_____
_____
_____
_____
_____
_____

Concerns I Have to Pray About

"Therefore, put on the full armor of GOD, so that when the day of evil comes, you may be able to stand your ground, and after you have done everything to stand."

Epshesians 6:13 (NIV)

Day 15

Taking a Stand

"Finally, my brethren, be strong in the Lord, and in the power of his might. Put on the whole armour of God, that ye may be able to stand against the wiles of the devil."

(Ephesians 6:10-11, King James Version)

Keep standing firm, trusting in the promises of God. Even in difficult times, we must stand firm.

Prayer:

Dear Heavenly Father,

Thank You for Your strength to stand today. I take a stand against all the workings of Satan that come to hinder Your perfect will for my life, my family, and my finances.

I stand on the truth of all Your promises. Your Word is settled in heaven. You watch over Your Word to perform it, as it is spoken out of my mouth.

You are active and alert. You hasten to perform Your Word. In the name of Jesus, I decree and declare all the promises of God over my body, soul, and mind.

I thank You, Lord, that when I am weak, you are strong within me. I do all things through Christ that strengthens me.

In Jesus' name,

Amen

Taking A Stand

Questions

_____
_____
_____
_____
_____
_____
_____

What God Revealed to Me

_____
_____
_____
_____
_____
_____
_____
_____

Scriptures

What God Revealed to Me

TAKING A STAND

Concerns I Have to Pray About

"There comes a moment when you must quit talking to God about the mountain in your life, and start talking to the mountain about your God."

-Mark Batterson

Day 16

Just Speak to It: Receiving the Promises from the Lord

"For verily I say unto you, That whosoever shall say unto this mountain, Be thou removed, and be thou cast into sea; and shall not doubt in his heart, but shall believe that those things which he saith shall come to pass; he shall have whatsoever he saith."

(Mark 11:23, King James Version)

Just speak to the situations and circumstances. Tell them the promises of God and what His Word declares. Persevere in your faith.

Prayer:

Heavenly Father,

I'm thankful for Your Word and all Your promises. All Your promises are yea and amen.

Today I begin to speak Your promises to every problem in my life that does not line up with Your perfect will. I speak and stand on the truth of Your word.

I speak to every mountain that the enemy has used against my family, my finances, my health, my career, and my job in the authority of Jesus' name. I command the mountains to be removed because with God all things are possible. Thank You, Father.

In Jesus' name,

Amen

JUST SPEAK TO IT:
RECEIVING THE PROMISES FROM THE LORD

Questions

_____
_____
_____
_____
_____
_____
_____

What God Revealed to Me

_____
_____
_____
_____
_____
_____
_____
_____

Scriptures

What God Revealed to Me

Just Speak to It:
Receiving the Promises from the Lord

Concerns I Have to Pray About

"With the Lord as your shepherd, you are truly cared for in every way."

-Charles Spurgeon

Day 17

Because You Are My Shepherd

"The LORD is my shepherd; I shall not want."

(Psalm 23:1, King James Version)

With God as my shepherd, I have everything I need.

Prayer:

Heavenly Father,

I thank You for being my shepherd, the God that watches over me and protects me. I thank You, Father, that as I seek Your kingdom first, everything that I need will be added unto me. I take no thought for what I'm going to eat because You supply my daily bread. I do not worry about what I should wear because You clothe me daily. Thank you for mercy, it's renewed every morning. Thank You for Your peace today. As I keep my mind stayed on You and all Your promises, I have perfect peace.

Thank You for Your grace that's here for me today. Thank You for Your joy; it gives me strength. Thank You for spiritual sight, so that I walk by faith and not by sight. I know all of my needs will be supplied.

In Jesus' name,

Amen

Questions

_____
_____
_____
_____
_____
_____
_____

What God Revealed to Me

_____
_____
_____
_____
_____
_____
_____
_____

30 Day Spiritual Warfare Prayer Journal

Scriptures

_____
_____
_____
_____
_____
_____

What God Revealed to Me

_____
_____
_____
_____
_____
_____
_____
_____

Concerns I Have to Pray About

"A habit of devout fellowship with GOD

is the spring of all our life,

and strength of it."

-Henry Edward Manning

Day 18

The Importance of True Fellowship

"God is faithful, by whom ye were called unto the fellowship of his Son Jesus Christ our Lord."
(1 Corinthians 1:9, King James Version)

What a blessing it is to have true fellowship with the Lord!

Prayer:

Dear Heavenly Father,

I thank You that You made provision, so we can have fellowship with You and get to know You in the power of the resurrection. So, I come, and I surrender all to You, withholding nothing, stripping off every fleshy thing that would hinder my fellowship and getting to know You.

Beginning with my mind. I dethrone my thoughts, and I put You on the throne of my mind. I welcome You, Holy Spirit, to usher me into fellowship with the Father.

Reveal every and anything in my life that will hinder the flow of the anointing that will bring me into His presence. Take all of me, Holy Spirit. I yield to you.

Fill me with all the fullness of You today. Thank You, Heavenly Father, for Your presence today and the power of Your Holy Spirit.

In Jesus' name,

Amen

THE IMPORTANCE OF TRUE FELLOWSHIP

Questions

What God Revealed to Me

Scriptures

What God Revealed to Me

Concerns I Have to Pray About

"For the Lord God is a son and shield, The Lord will give grace and glory: no good thing will he withhold from them that walk uprightly."

-Psalms 84:11

Day 19

Walking in the Blessings and Living in the Blessings

"That the blessing of Abraham might come on the Gentiles through Jesus Christ; that we might receive the promise of the Spirit through faith."

(Galatians 3:14, King James Version)

To be blessed or happy, our hope and confidence must be in God. Trust in God and all His promises and blessings.

Prayer:

Dear Heavenly Father,

I thank You for Your blessings for this day. As I go through this day, I thank You for all Your blessings, and I declare them for this day. I thank You that I'm "blessed in the city; I'm blessed in the field" and in my surroundings.

I am blessed. I thank You that the fruit of my body, my children, are blessed; my cupboards are blessed. I'm blessed to be going out today. I'm blessed that the work of my hands is blessed today.

I thank You that my blessings are running me down and taking over in every area of my life. I thank You that I am the head and not the tail. I am a lender and not a borrower.

I thank You, Father, that my life is blessed today. My mind is blessed, and I am walking in all the blessings of Deuteronomy 28. I decree and declare them.

In Jesus' name,

Amen

Questions

What God Revealed to Me

Scriptures

What God Revealed to Me

Concerns I Have to Pray About

"GOD changes caterpillars into butterflies, sand into pearls, coals into diamonds using time and pressure. He's working on you too."

-Rick Warren

Day 20

Being Made Whole in His Presence

"Thou wilt shew me the path of life: in thy presence is fullness of joy; at thy right hand there are pleasures for evermore."

(Psalm 16:11, King James Version)

If we stay in God's presence, worshiping Him in spirit and in truth, we will experience His peace, joy, and wholeness.

Prayer:

Heavenly Father,

I thank You for Your son, Jesus, and for the shedding of His blood and the work of Calvary's cross. He has made it possible for me to come into Your presence.

So, I come today with a grateful heart, realizing that in Your presence I can receive fullness of joy. In Your presence, I can be naked and not ashamed. So, I ask You to make me whole. Here is my heart, and here is my soul. I surrender all to You.

Today, Lord, I believe. Help my unbelief. Strengthen my faith to be made whole and complete in every area of my life. Deliver me from all my hidden faults and presumptuous sins. I thank You, Heavenly Father, for making me whole in Your presence today.

In Jesus' name,

Amen

Questions

What God Revealed to Me

30 Day Spiritual Warfare Prayer Journal

Scriptures

_____
_____
_____
_____
_____
_____

What God Revealed to Me

_____
_____
_____
_____
_____
_____
_____
_____

Concerns I Have to Pray About

"Cast your burden on the Lord, and he will sustain you, he will never permit the righteous to be moved."

(Psalms 55:22, New King James Version)

Day 21

Prayer of Release

"Verily I say unto you, Whatsoever ye shall bind on earth shall be bound in heaven: and whatsoever ye shall loose on earth shall be loosed in heaven."

(Matthew 18:18, King James Version)

We have been given authority by Jesus Christ to bind and to loose with the power in our tongues and to speak and release the answers for our prayers.

Prayer:

Heavenly Father,

I thank You for Your son, Jesus, and the power of Your Holy Spirit. He has given unto us the keys to the kingdom. The authority to release what belongs to us is through his name.

I thank You that we are seated with Christ in the heavenly realm because we are united with Him (Ephesians 2:6). Therefore, this day, in the authority of Jesus' name, I command every blessing that belongs to me and my family to be released. I command every answer that is held up by the enemy to be released in Jesus' name.

I bind every demonic and evil force that has been set up against me. Every spirit has no power to hinder my spiritual walk, my health, my wealth, and every spiritual gift that God has placed within me. I command you to go in Jesus' name. No weapon formed against me shall prosper. Father, I thank You that today I decree and declare release over my life, my family, and all that belongs to me.

In Jesus' name,

Amen

PRAYER OF RELEASE

Questions

What God Revealed to Me

Scriptures

What God Revealed to Me

PRAYER OF RELEASE

Concerns I Have to Pray About

"When your drive is moving your purpose, focus must hold the wheels, else you might miss the way. And do you know what that means? Avoid crash!!! Stay focus!"

-Israelmore Ayivor

Day 22

Staying Focused

"Thou wilt keep him in perfect peace; whose mind is stayed on thee: because he trusteth in thee."

(Isaiah 26:3, King James Version)

To stay focused on God, we must saturate and flood our minds with His Word.

Prayer:

Heavenly Father,

I thank You for Your Word that You have given to me this day. I flood my mind with Your Word that I may stay focused on all Your promises as I pray, as I worship, and adore You.

Bring every unholy thought into captivity with Your Word, casting down every imagination with Your Word. Bring every thought into captivity to the obedience of Christ.

I ask You to keep my mind, so I will experience Your perfect peace today in every situation that I may encounter, knowing that I already have the victory because I am focused on what Your Word declares.

So today, I will not allow things, people, or situations to make me lose my focus. I keep my eyes upon You, the Author and Finisher of my faith. I thank You.

In Jesus' name,

Amen

STAYING FOCUSED

Questions

What God Revealed to Me

Scriptures

_____

_____

_____

_____

_____

_____

What God Revealed to Me

_____

_____

_____

_____

_____

_____

_____

_____

Concerns I Have to Pray About

"Finally my brethren be strong in the Lord, and in power of his might. Put on the whole armour of GOD, that ye may be able to stand against the wiles of the devil."

-Ephesians 6:10-11

Day 23

Being and Staying Militant: Ready for Battle

"Finally, my brethren, be strong in the Lord, and in the power of his might."

(Ephesians 6:10, King James Version)

To be spiritually militant, we have to be wakeful, watchful, spiritually alert, praying aggressively.

Prayer:

Dear Heavenly Father,

I thank You for Your power today being used with all the fullness of the Holy Spirit. I yield to You, Holy Spirit. You are the warrior that lives inside of me. You are my help. So, I ask You to empower me to pray aggressively. Open my spiritual eyes that I may be watchful and discern the tactics of the enemy. Awaken my spirit that I will become alert and aware of the wicked devices of the enemy.

Help me to stand fast in the faith, using every piece of my spiritual armor. I hold up the shield of faith against every fiery dart that the enemy brings against me, in Jesus' name.

I will be militant, and I will be alert. My spirit will be awakened by the power of the Holy Spirit. The warrior within me will arise and wage war against every evil force that's directed towards me. I am a soldier in the army of the Lord.

In Jesus' name,

Amen

Being and Staying Militant: Ready for Battle

Questions

What God Revealed to Me

30 Day Spiritual Warfare Prayer Journal

Scriptures

What God Revealed to Me

Concerns I Have to Pray About

"If we live in the spirit, let us also walk in the spirit."

-Galatians 5:25

Day 24

Walking in Pureness of Heart by the Power of the Holy Spirit

"Blessed are the pure in heart: for they shall see God."

(Matthew 5:8, King James Version)

I walk in pureness of heart. We cannot allow evil, jealousy, envy, strife, or unforgiveness to take root in our hearts. None of the works of the flesh must be allowed either.

Prayer:

Dear Heavenly Father,

Thank You for knowing me. You know my uprising and my down sitting. You know my thoughts afar off. I come before You, today, asking You to create in me a clean heart and renew a right spirit within me. Do not let the flow of the Holy Spirit be grieved in any way.

Bring into the light anything in my heart that is not pleasing to You. Help me to remain pure before You, to lift up holy hands and a pure heart. Father, You are the Creator.

Give me a heart after You, Father, that I may love right and follow Your statutes and keep Your commandments. Today, I give my heart to You to purify. My desire is to walk before You with a pure heart and a right spirit.

In order for me to see You, I must be pure in heart. I can only be pure in heart through the power of the Holy Spirit that abides within me. I thank You, Father, for purifying my heart today and for revealing my heart to me. I walk in pureness of heart.

In Jesus' name,

Amen

**WALKING IN PURENESS OF HEART
BY THE POWER OF THE HOLY SPIRIT**

Questions

What God Revealed to Me

Scriptures

_____
_____
_____
_____
_____
_____
_____

What God Revealed to Me

_____
_____
_____
_____
_____
_____
_____
_____
_____

***Walking in Pureness of Heart
by the Power of the Holy Spirit***

Concerns I Have to Pray About

"Be on your guard, stand firm in the faith,

be courageous, be strong."

-I Corinthians 16:13 NIV

Day 25

Taking a Stand in the Midst of Adversity

"For in the time of trouble he shall hide me in his pavilion: in the secret of his tabernacle shall he hide me; he shall set me up upon a rock."

(Psalm 27:5, King James Version)

In the times of adversity, we must trust God for the strength to take us through; and we must rely on His promise to deliver us.

Prayer:

Dear Heavenly Father,

You are my refuge and my strong tower. In Your name is safety. Today, no matter the adversity I'm facing, I will not be overtaken by discouragement for You are the God of all hope in the midst of trouble.

You shall revive me. I put on Your strength, and Your courage. I lean and depend on Your blessed Holy Spirit to equip me with all I need to stand and be strong in the power of His might.

When I am weak, then, You are strong within me. I thank You, Father, for Your grace. I receive Your grace because it is sufficient enough to take me through all I'm facing. I know that I'm not alone; You are with me, and You are here to help me and to uphold me with the right hand of Your righteousness.

I will not drown in the midst of this. Having done all to stand, I stand with the sword of Your Word and the shield of faith. I am victorious through Jesus Christ, my Savior.

Thank You Jesus,

Amen

TAKING A STAND IN THE MIDST OF ADVERSITY

Questions

_____
_____
_____
_____
_____
_____
_____

What God Revealed to Me

_____
_____
_____
_____
_____
_____
_____
_____

Scriptures

What God Revealed to Me

Taking a Stand in the Midst of Adversity

Concerns I Have to Pray About

"Be strong and courageous for the Lord your GOD is with you."

-Joshua 1:9

Day 26

Taking Courage

"Be strong and of good courage, fear not, nor be afraid of them: for the Lord thy God, he it is that doth go with thee; he will not fail thee, nor forsake thee."

(Deuteronomy 31:6, King James Version)

Jesus encourages many people in the Bible to take courage, regarding their circumstances, and not to fear. He is still speaking to us today saying, "Take courage. Do not be overtaken by fear."

Prayer:

Dear Heavenly Father,

You have not given us the spirit of fear but of power and love and a sound mind. Today, I take courage in every circumstance. I take courage in knowing that You are my healer, Jehovah Rapha. I take courage in knowing that You are Jehovah Shalom, my peace.

You are everything I need You to be. You are the "I AM" in my life. I ask You, Heavenly Father, to help me to be strong and to be diligent.

Fill me with Your power and might because You have girded me with strength for the day. You, O Lord, are a shield for me, my glory and the one who lifts up my head.

I will trust in You. I take courage, and I put on the strength of God. I will not fear for You are with me. I am encouraged in the Lord and by His power. I will rejoice and be glad.

In Jesus' name,

Amen

Questions

What God Revealed to Me

Scriptures

What God Revealed to Me

Concerns I Have to Pray About

"The Lord himself will fight for you,

just stay calm."

-Exodus 14:14 NLT

Day 27

Staying Calm

"Be ye angry, and sin not: let not the sun go down upon your wrath."

(John 4:24, King James Version)

• •

To remain calm in difficult situations is being controlled by the power of the Holy Spirit. He is controlling our tongues.

Prayer:

Dear Heavenly Father,

I thank You for this day. I thank You that You are in control of everything that happens today. I surrender my entire being to You.

Take control of my mouth. Bridle my tongue and keep the door of my mouth. Let my words be edifying to the hearers and be words of encouragement. Help me not to react to any situation in anger. Keep me calm, knowing that You are in control.

You are not a God of confusion, but You are a God of peace. Search my heart. In the name of Jesus, I bind every stronghold of the enemy.

Today, I surrender my emotions to You, yielding to the power of the Holy Spirit. I will be swift to hear and slow to speak. The words that I speak will be words of encouragement and not defeat, words of life and not death.

I thank You, Father, for keeping watch over my mouth, allowing me to give You thanks and keeping a continued praise on my lips. Let the words of my mouth and the meditation of my heart be acceptable in thy sight, O Lord, my strength, and my redeemer (Psalms 19:14, KJV).

Thank You, Heavenly Father. By the power of the Holy Spirit, I will praise You with joyful lips and a pure heart.

In Jesus' name, Amen.

Staying Calm

Questions

What God Revealed to Me

Scriptures

What God Revealed to Me

STAYING CALM

Concerns I Have to Pray About

"For I will pour out water on the thirsty land and streams on the dry ground. I will pour my spirit on your offspring and my blessings on your descendents."

-Isaiah 44:3

Day 28

Receiving A Fresh Outpouring of Your Spirit

"And it shall come to pass afterward; that I will pour out my spirit upon all flesh; and your sons and your daughters shall prophesy, your old men shall dream dreams, your young men shall see visions."

(Joel 2:28, King James Version)

There is always more for us in our relationship with God. Deep calleth to deep. God is calling us to a higher place in Him to experience a fresh outpouring of His Spirit upon us. To receive it, we must seek and worship Him wholeheartedly with all our minds and souls.

Prayer:

Heavenly Father,

As I come before You, I worship and adore You. You are worthy to be praised, and there is none like unto thee. As I come before You, fill me with a fresh outpouring of Your spirit. As the heart panteth after the water brooks so panteth my soul after thee O God. I long for more of You. As I worship You, come quench this thirsting in my soul. I need a refreshing of Your anointing to overshadow me, as rivers of living waters flow through me.

Make me, mold me into what You will have me to be. You are the potter, and I am the clay. Help me Holy Spirit to become pliable in the Father's hand as I go along my way continuing to experience Your love and peace. Allow it to flow from within to reach others that come cross my path: to encourage, to witness, and share my faith to those who are broken in heart and wounded in spirit. I can only do this through the power of Your Holy Spirit. I thank You, Father.

In Jesus' name,

Amen

Questions

What God Revealed to Me

Scriptures

What God Revealed to Me

Concerns I Have to Pray About

"May you be strengthened with all power according to his glorious might, for all endurance and patience with joy."

-Colossians 1:11

Day 29

Knowing God in the Power of His Might

"Finally, my brethren, be strong in the Lord, and in the power of his might."

(Ephesians 6:10, King James Version)

....

Know God and the power of God's might. We must be strong in God's strength not our own by putting on the whole armor and the power of His might.

Prayer:

Dear Heavenly Father,

I thank You for Your armor that you have given me. I ask You to strengthen the inner man with the power of God's might that I will be able to withstand the wiles of the enemy. I realize that I wrestle not against flesh and blood. This is a spiritual battle. God, You are mighty.

Satan, I rebuke you in the authority of Jesus' name. Today, I triumph over you in the strength of His name and in the power of His might that is working on the inside of me.

Satan, I rebuke you In the name of Jesus. Today, I take authority over you in the power of Jesus' name and in the power of His might that abides within me this day. I have victory over you. In Jesus' name, you will not cause me to be discouraged or deceived me in any way. I thank You, Father, for the power of Your might in every situation today.

In Jesus' name

Amen

Questions

What God Revealed to Me

30 Day Spiritual Warfare Prayer Journal

Scriptures

_____

_____

_____

_____

_____

_____

_____

What God Revealed to Me

_____

_____

_____

_____

_____

_____

_____

_____

Concerns I Have to Pray About

"I have set the Lord always before me,

because he is at my right hand

I will not be shaken."

-Psalms 16:8

Day 30

Being Persistent in Spiritual Warfare During Trials

"Continue in prayer, and watch in the same with thanksgiving."

(Colossians 4:2, King James Version)

We need to be persistent in prayer, always declaring unto God His promises, praying until something happens, and pushing through the trials until change takes place.

Prayer:

Dear Heavenly Father,

I thank You for Your Son, Jesus. I thank You for the work of the cross. I come boldly to Your throne of grace, decreeing and declaring Your promises.

Today, I take a stand against all the works of the enemy. I thank You that You have given me power over the enemy, and nothing shall by any means harm me. I thank You that You have given me the power to tread on serpents, scorpions, and over all power of the enemy, and nothing shall by any means harm me.

I persistently call upon Your name to help me during the trials for You are my helper, my defense, my refuge, and my strong tower. Thank You for the power of Your name because it is a strong tower. I can run into it, and I am safe.

I take Your Word as my sword, my faith as a shield, and I lean and depend on the power of the Holy Spirit to uphold me and guide me through this trial. I know that weeping may endure for a night, but joy comes to me this day.

I have the victory through Jesus Christ, my Lord and Savior. I will praise You with joyful praise and bless Your holy name for You are faithful.

In Jesus' name,

Amen

BEING PERSISTENT IN SPIRITUAL WARFARE DURING TRIALS

Questions

What God Revealed to Me

Scriptures

What God Revealed to Me

Being Persistent in Spiritual Warfare During Trials

Concerns I Have to Pray About

About the Author

Dr. Priscilla Akins is a native of Margaretta, Florida. Prayer is and always has been a vital part of her life. The first church she joined was the New Jerusalem Church of God in Christ, under the pastorate of Elder Mack Ruise. She became an active member of the Baker County Prayer Band, which was founded and led by her mother, Missionary Lonnie Bell Lampkins. Her mother was also responsible for prayer being birthed into her life at an early age.

The Baker County Prayer Band traveled throughout Baker County and nearby counties doing the work of the Lord, witnessing the sick being healed, the lame walking, cancer and all manner of diseases being healed, and souls saved, delivered, and set free.

Obedience to God brought her to accept her first calling as a missionary at New Jerusalem Church of God in Christ. In 1986, the Holy Spirit led her to Orlando, Florida. Under the leadership of Bishop Henry Leonard at Tabernacle of the Enlightened Church of God, she accepted the call of exhorter, minister, and evangelist. She was later appointed as president of the Prayer Band and State Evangelist, traveling and conducting revivals throughout Florida and abroad. For the past thirty-six years, she has served as a faithful prayer warrior of the Prophetic Prayer Ministry, founded by Prophetess Brenda Williams of Orlando, Florida.

After years of traveling and ministering in Orlando, Florida, being led by the Holy Spirit, Dr. Akins returned to her native home of Baker County, Florida. In 1994, Dr. Akins established Word of Life Ministries Outreach. For sixteen years, the ministry conducted an annual forty-night prayer and fasting consecration. Pastor Dorothy Ford, Dr Akins's sister, worked side by side with Dr. Akins, providing meals for the homeless through the soup kitchen, offering clothing, and for a few years, even provided childcare for needy families in the community. Also, during her sixteen-year tenure, she provided free counseling and established the Word of Life Ministries daily prayer line for those in need of prayer or counseling.

In 1995, Word of Life Ministry merged with Worldwide Kingdom Ministries, led by Bishop Milton Perry of New York. After being ordained as overseer by Bishop Brown and Bishop Martin of Jacksonville, Florida, Dr. Akins taught discipleship to leadership courses, and students were ordained after successful completion of the courses. In 2008, a merger with Fellowship Churches United, under the covering of Bishop Gracie Jackson of Augusta, Georgia led her to serving in the prayer ministry and an appointment to Prayer Ambassador.

After receiving her Master of Divinity degree from Lahori Bible Institute, she became an instructor with Lahori Bible Institute, completed the School of the Prophets, and received her Doctor of Divinity degree. Returning to her native home, she began fellowshipping with Living Word Outreach Ministry, pastored by Pastor Sammie L. Daniels in Lake City, Florida and served as overseer for three years. In 2014, New Hope Outreach Deliverance Ministry in Jacksonville, Florida was established by Dr. Akins. She currently serves as the intercessor of Global Ministries International under Presiding Prelate Bishop, Alva D. Harris, of Deliverance Temple Global Ministries, which is also pastored by his wife, Pastor Ida Harris.

On a more personal note, Dr. Priscilla Akins and her husband conceived four beautiful girls, one who has passed away. Currently, Dr. Akins and her three daughters, their families, and eleven grandchildren reside in northeast Florida.

Our Prayer Ministry

Dr. Priscilla Akins Prayer Ministries

Call in Prayer Line

Every Monday night @ 9 p.m.
1(612) 421-0949
Code: 197971

Every Monday, Wednesday, and Friday @ 6a.m.
1(605) 475-3235
Code: 608423

Contact the Author

You are welcome to email or write the author with comments about this book. You are also welcome to contact her for bookings. Dr. Akins is available for book club presentations, book signings, or speaking engagements for your group or organization (conferences, workshops, retreats, seminars, women's groups, women's ministries and women's clubs).

Email:
priscillaakins12@gmail.com

Connect with her on social media:

Facebook:
https://www.facebook.com/priscilla.akins.9

Notes

www.ingramcontent.com/pod-product-compliance
Lightning Source LLC
Chambersburg PA
CBHW071437080526
44587CB00014B/1888